Heaven On Earth

Unlocking the Power of Prayer

Kim Robbins, M.Div

Paperback ISBN: 979-8-9909952-0-8
eBook ISBN: 979-8-9909952-1-5

Kim Robbins Ministries
2095 Hwy 211 NW, Suite 2-F #306
Braselton, GA 30517
www.kimrobbins.org

Printed in the United States of America
First Edition 2024

For more information, email admin@kimrobbins.org

Dedication

O God, you are my God; earnestly I seek you; my soul thirsts for you; my flesh faints for you, as in a dry and weary land where there is no water. – Psalm 63:1 (ESV)

Prayer is the slender nerve that moves the muscle of omnipotence. – Charles Spurgeon

Contents

Preface

Have you ever felt like your prayers only traveled as far as your ceiling? That they sometimes seem to fall back down, hitting you right in the face. Perhaps you thought that maybe you should go and pray outside so they would rise a little higher – to reach heaven quicker. LOL

At some time or another we've all felt that our prayers weren't being heard . . . never mind not even getting answered! We pray and pray, but things don't seem to change. We chalk it up as though God is saying "no," or "maybe." We think that He might be teaching us a lesson in patience — "waiting" for our answer. We compare ourselves to Daniel, who waited 21 days for an answer to prayer. It must be the devil and his demons that are blocking our "yes" from God. Does any of this seem familiar?

I admit, some prayers do take time to manifest; like the salvation of a loved one, for example. But, sometime back, God began to answer almost every prayer I prayed. There were times when I could hardly get it out of my mouth before He answered! I was definitely in the "favor flow" and cannot necessarily attribute anything I did to help bring those prayers to fruition.

However, having my prayers answered created in me a desire to want others to experience those same responses to their prayers, even if favor isn't involved. Not every prayer is always like that; but, I asked God to show me, through His Word, what causes Him to answer prayer. This book is what He gave me. The simple, short, and easy to read style has been done intentionally. Some books have so many pages that our problem is solved or we tire of reading before the book is completed. Prayer is much more simple sometimes than we make it (as are other biblical subjects). My goal is to help you in every area in the shortest amount of time. I want you to see your desires in prayer manifest sooner, rather than later. I believe this book will radically transform your prayer life, if you take to heart what is shared here.

While this book is simple and short, and could easily be read in one day, (and I want your prayers coming to fruition soon), it is meant to be digested more slowly. I encourage you to use this as a 12 day or 12 week journey. It can be used for a prayer devotional book or for small group study as well.

Because I believe in the power of prayer and the principles shared in this book, I believe you will have "praise reports" to share for the prayers God has answered. And we want to know about them. You can log onto www.kimrobbins.org and share them on our *Contact* page (www.kimrobbins.org/share-your-story), e-mail us at **admin@kimrobbins.org**, or write to us at **2095 Hwy. 211 NW, Suite 2-F #306, Braselton, GA 30517.**. Now, set your heart for success, get ready to pray, and watch God move mountains and bring down Heaven on your behalf!

Introduction

In a world that continues to unfold in a spiral of never-ending chaos and corruption, the need for powerful, effective prayer – that can cause lives to be saved and transformed, governments to be shifted, minds to be apprehended to the leading of the Spirit, miracles to happen, and invoke the very presence of God's glory to manifest – is absolutely necessary! Prayer is our direct line of communication with God – the most powerful medium through which heaven's influence can descend upon the earth. Heaven comes down to earth when effective prayers push their way towards God's throne. We used to say "when praises go up, blessings come down." But I'd like to offer this thought: "when prayers go up, heaven comes down!"

You still might be wondering, "Why another book on prayer though?" I had a similar thought when I asked the Lord what book He would like me to write. I knew that God wanted me to write but I wasn't sure where to start. After the directive to write a prayer book I realized that everything in our lives, and especially as it pertains to God's Kingdom, begins with prayer. So, why shouldn't that be the first book? (This is the revision of that book). But why *another* prayer book? What more can we possibly learn about prayer? We know prayer is powerful. We understand it's how we communicate with God. So, what more can we learn? I like to look at it this way: First of all, you can never get too much of a good thing, right? LOL But also, there are "layers" of learning from the Word of God. Have you ever read a scripture, understood it, applied it to your life and later when you read it again you gather a new understanding? Or, see the scripture differently than you had previously? This is what I mean by "layers." We can always learn something new!

That's what I believe will happen with this book. You will learn something about prayer that perhaps you hadn't really thought about before or applied to your life. The perspective within these pages will help as a guide not only on the 'how' but the 'why' and 'what for' of prayer.

My goal is to help you unlock the potential of prayer in your life. This is an invitation to rediscover the richness of prayer, offering insights and practical guidance to cause your prayers to not be just words, but a force that compels God to answer and can shape the very fabric of our lives, both present and future. Prayer is not some obligation or ritualistic activity; it is a conversation with the Creator of the Universe and the Savior of our souls. It is an exchange that breathes life into our hopes and dreams. It is the lifeline that connects us to the Source and transforms our struggles into successes, our troubles into triumphs, and our moments of despair into beacons of hope.

This book delves into the need for and value of prayer—revealing that it's not just about asking, but about aligning our hearts with God's will, allowing heaven to manifest in our lives here on earth. It is a guide to complement your journey to effective prayer. Prayer empowers us to "co-create" with God. In the following pages I believe you will come into a deeper understanding of prayer's significance and be weaponized to pray with intention, conviction, and, most importantly, effectiveness.

How do we pray with purpose? How do we tap into the transformative power that lies within these precious times with the Lord? Like the musical group Lakeside used to sing, "come along and ride on [*this*] fantastic voyage," and let us unlock together the gates through which heaven may come down to earth.

In prayer it is better to have a heart without words, than words without a heart.

— John bunyan

Very early in the morning, while it was still dark, Jesus got up, left the house and went off to a solitary place, where he prayed.

— Mark 1:35, NIV

CHAPTER 1

Matters of the Heart

You will seek me and find me when you seek me with all
your heart. (Jer. 29:13, NIV)

. . . the Lord looks on the heart. (1 Sam. 16:7b, NIV)

B efore we get into some of the principles that govern
effective, successful prayer, we must first understand the
matters of the heart. If our heart is not right and we're not
praying for the "right" reasons none of the things I'm about
to share will even matter because they will not come to
fruition if they aren't coming from a place of genuine
sincerity. Psalm 66:18 (KJV)says that "*if I regard iniquity in*
my heart, the Lord will not hear me." Did you know that
God does not hear the prayers of a sinner? John 9:31 (NASB)
says that " . . . . *God does not hear sinners; but if anyone is*
God-fearing and does His will, He hears him." God hears
the "sinner's prayer" but He doesn't hear the prayer of one
who is living in sin. In other words, He hears the prayer for
the cry of salvation but scripture tells us that He does not
hear the prayer of (meaning He won't listen or answer)

someone who is unrepentant and has sin in his heart. Our hearts must be right before God when coming to Him in prayer.

Jesus tells us to love God with our whole heart, and love others the same way we love ourselves. When we love God and love others we are prepared to begin our journey into powerful answered prayer. The state of our heart tells God our intentions, motives, and depth of compassion for others and our desire to see His will come to pass.

Let's back up just a minute and discuss prayer, in general. What is prayer exactly? In basic fundamental terms, prayer is a time of request and petition to the Lord for the things we desire to see come to pass. But it is also a time of worship, praise, and adoration of the Lord. When Jesus was teaching the disciples how to pray He began with "Our Father, who is in Heaven, Holy is your name." This is an acknowledgment of who God is, where His rulership operates from, and the purity and righteousness that makes up the entirety of His being. Jesus ended His instruction with "for Yours is the Kingdom, and the power, and the glory forever" (Matthew 6:13, NIV). Again, we acknowledge God's sovereignty, power, authority, and the glory that belongs to Him. If we never make a petition or request from God, we are still operating in prayer when we spend time simply exalting and praising God. We need to spend time expressing our gratitude and adoration for the Lord. We also need to recognize His holiness, and His power, and glorify

Him. God does not have an ego. But acknowledging Him puts our hearts in the right place to receive an answer to our prayer. Part of prayer is stopping to take time out of our busy lives, or before our days even get busy, to honor God, commune with Him, and thank Him for all He's done and will do. When our hearts are right before the Lord, He will incline His ear to hear our requests. We don't, however, pour out accolades only to obtain answers to these requests. This would be operating with an incorrect and selfish motive. We are simply loving on God and whether He answers our prayers or not we continue to extol and revere Him.

Let's think about it in terms of our own humanity. If you were going to ask someone for something, you're more likely to receive it if 1) they know you love them, and 2) they know you aren't saying nice things just to get something. How would you feel if someone only called on you when they wanted something? I'm pretty sure you wouldn't get very excited when they call. Relationships must be developed, nurtured, and respected. When this kind of communication goes well between people then trust is developed. When we have trust in our relationships we are more likely to give to others when they ask. It is the same with God. As you develop your relationship with Him He will be able to trust you with the answer to your petition. Another way to look at it is that as you build your relationship with the Lord you will be more able to hear His answer to your prayer or the direction He is telling you to go, or not go, or whatever is needed for that request to be fulfilled.

Whatever the case, God knows the intentions of our heart. While we acknowledge and exalt Him, thank Him, and show our love for God, we can't come to Him with simple "lip service." The Word even talks about this in Isaiah 29:13 (ESV) "And the Lord said, '*Because this people draw near with their mouth and honor me with their lips, while their hearts are far from me . . .*" We must speak to Him from our heart. Our intentions should be to love Him and thank Him from a place of authenticity and gratitude that we have for who He is and all He has done. We should exalt Him and give praise to Him before we begin lifting up our petitions, requests, or desires to God for Him to answer.

One way to begin honoring the Lord, if you're not familiar with prayer, is to speak His Word. For example, I often start my morning prayers with "Lord, I thank you that your mercies are new every morning." This comes from Lamentations 3:22-23 (ESV): *"The steadfast love of the Lord never ceases, his mercies never come to an end; they are new every morning; great is your faithfulness."* This is also the scripture I believe for one of the most famous and beautiful hymns ever written, "Great Is Thy Faithfulness."

God says that His Word always accomplishes, or fulfills, its intended purpose. Isaiah 55:10-11(ESV) says *"For as the rain and the snow come down from heaven and do not return there but water the earth, making it bring forth and* *sprout, giving seed to the sower and bread to the eater, <u>so shall my word be that goes out from my mouth; it shall not return to me empty, but it shall accomplish that which I purpose, and shall succeed in the thing for which I sent it*</u>* (emphasis mine). God sees to it that His Word achieves whatever He sent it forth to do. So, praying the Word is a great way to start magnifying the Lord as well as to know that the answer to our prayer is on its way and it will happen according to God's Word. I'll discuss more on that later.

Back to the heart issue. Part of making sure our heart is right, and that we have the right motives, is to pray for others. After we have spent time in worship, praise, and adoration of the Lord, our focus should not immediately turn to our own issues (though sometimes this can be quite challenging). If we look and think hard enough I'm sure we can find someone who is in a worse situation than ours and in need of answered prayer. After loving God, we need to love others by lifting up our prayers to God on their behalf. Compassion for others is a large part of having that prayer answered. We may be their only hope for having that situation turn in their favor. More powerful than that is how having a compassionate heart can bring salvation and eternal life to someone else! We must pray for others to come to know the Lord as their Savior and for them to allow Him to be Lord over their life. Our prayers can bring them to salvation.

I've seen this happen in my own life. I prayed for the salvation of many friends and family members. At first, I felt like my prayers just weren't bringing forth the fruit I was expecting. While not everything was exactly as I had hoped, many friends and family members progressed in their spiritual life. Some didn't believe in God and now they do. Others believed but never attended church and they started going. One cousin in particular, for whom I had been praying for off and on for at least 15 years or more, had been heavily involved in New Age. He recently came fully into his relationship with Jesus and is publicly sharing his testimony. I'm sure I haven't been the only one praying for him but I love seeing prayers of the lost come to fruition, and in such a powerful and impactful way! Genuine love and compassion for others (not for pity or for personal gain) and to glorify God are just the start of prayers that manifest on earth what is already done in heaven!

So, let's search our hearts and come to God in truth and get ready to build on that foundation. Let the journey begin of sending up sincere, "heartfelt" prayers that cause heaven to come down!

Live Out Loud

Prayer:

Heavenly Father, Create in me a clean heart and renew a right spirit in me. Search my heart, Lord. If it's not where it should be, please forgive me and cleanse me from all unrighteousness. Forgive my complacency with prayer. I will guard my heart and keep it focused on your will.. I want to be pleasing to you and I want my prayers to be answered in order to bless others and glorify you. Amen

Action:

Matthew chapter 6, verse 21 (NIV) says that "where your treasure is, there will your heart be also." We've been discussing how important it is to make sure our hearts are right before we even begin the process of praying effectively. Take a moment and find out where your treasure lies. Ask the Lord to search your heart and take the time to reflect. Make adjustments where necessary so you can move forward into a powerful prayer life.

Psalm 57:7, KJV > *My heart is fixed, O God, my heart is fixed: I will sing and give praise.*

Pr. 27:19, KJV > *As in water face answers to face, so the heart of man to man.*

List 3 things God has done in your life for which you are grateful:

1. _____

2. _____

3. _____

Write down your "take-a-ways" from this lesson on Matters of the Heart:

_____

_____

_____

_____

_____

Man was created on the sixth day so that he could not be boastful, since he came after the flea in the order of creation.

— Haggadah

When you have nothing left but God, then for the first time you become aware that God is enough.

— Maude Royden

CHAPTER 2

Recognize Your Need for Prayer

And to Seth, to him also there was born a son; and he
called his name Enos: then began men to call upon the
name of the Lord. (Genesis 4:26, KJV)

Since the very beginning of creation God always intended
to have a relationship with mankind. In Genesis we read
that He walked with Adam in the cool of the day. In other
words, He fellowshipped with "them" (Adam & Eve) in the
Garden. Obviously, since God and man communed and
conversed on a regular basis, there was no need for "prayer,"
as we know it today. It wasn't until after Adam and Eve fell
into sin and separated themselves from the presence of God
that there arose the need for prayer. God could no longer be
in their midst because He is a Holy God and Adam and Eve
would not have been able to endure His presence. So, did
they continue to talk to God? If so, how did they do it since
He no longer walked with them in the garden? Though we
see that God spoke to Cain about his brother and Cain spoke
back to the Lord, the Bible actually makes no other mention

of them or anyone petitioning God, or praying to Him, until the birth of Adam and Eve's grandson, Enos.

Enos was the son of Seth, the third son of Adam and Eve, through whom the lineage of Jesus would come. Cain and Abel were their first two sons; but Cain, having killed his younger brother Abel, was sent away. With one son deceased, and the other marked because of what he had done, Seth was now the beginning of God's restorative process. From the very start, God was initiating a plan to reconnect with mankind. While He had to separate Himself from sin, God was still working to reestablish His close fellowship with us.

Genesis 4:26 (KJV) says, *"To Seth also a son was born, and he called his name Enosh (or Enos). At that time people began to call upon the name of the Lord."* So, they called on God (i.e. prayed) after Enos was born. From the creation of Adam to the birth of Seth, his 3rd son, was 130 years. From the birth of Seth to the birth of Enos was 105 years. We can see here that at minimum it was more than 105 years before mankind began to "call upon" God. I wondered why the Bible mentioned Enos. What was the significance of his name? Why didn't they call on God sooner? Why wasn't another name mentioned? Why Enos?

I decided to look up the meaning of the name Enos to see if I could gain insight into these questions. The name Enos, interestingly, means *mortal.* Mortal, of course, is defined as "a human being subject to death, often contrasted with a divine being." Definitely don't want to name a kid Enos! But I believe there's some significance here to understanding prayer. Adam and Eve had walked with God, lived in the Garden, been in His Presence. They had been "divinely created." They had only known life, peace, joy, and immortality, until the Fall. They experienced death with their son Abel, and their firstborn was sent out from them. Now they were faced with a choice with their third child. They named him Seth, meaning "anointed and appointed." Wow, what a great name! He was appointed by God to be the person through whom God would restore His relationship with mankind. The first thing Seth does with the birth of his son, the next in line towards the arrival of the Savior, is give him a name that brings awareness of where mankind is and where his relationship lies with God. Mankind is now *enos*, mortal and subject to death, until he is rescued by the Divine and given immortality, "the ability to live forever; eternal life."

Thus, man began to call upon God, (i.e. to pray) when he realized his *mortality; his enos*. He knew, no matter how many years he lived on the Earth, that he would eventually die. This is a great place to start in prayer! Humility! We must realize our mortality and humble ourselves to the Immortal One. As noted before, it took man between 105 and 235 years to recognize this! But they did eventually realize the finite state of humanity. Perhaps the inability to live in an eternal state (as was God's original intent) caused

21

man to reach for the immortal. Because we were created in the image of God, we retained the desire to be attached and connected to the Eternal and Immortal Source. Though it was many years after the Fall, man began to recognize the *need* for communication with his Creator. No longer able to commune or fellowship with the Lord in the Garden, man's inner parts yearned for the reestablishment of a relationship with God (much like we do today). So, they began to "call upon God."

Christians often go for extended periods of time without talking with God, reading the Word, or attending church before they realize they must reconnect. Why is that? Perhaps it is because sometimes we think ourselves to be invincible, immortal, and "able to leap tall buildings in a single bound." If you know a teenager you know someone who believes they can do anything, go anywhere, and live young forever. Then somewhere along the way reality hits. Just like Seth realized the immortality of man and that we must reconnect with God, we too must come to the realization that we have a *need* for prayer. Then we pray.

Before any prayer can be answered, before God will grant our petition or request, and after our hearts are right in coming to Him, we must recognize our *need* to have fellowship with God. Life has no meaning without a relationship with God. Our purpose in life is to reconnect with our Creator. Our sins are forgiven through the sacrificial offering of Jesus and the fullness of a relationship with God comes through constant fellowship with Him.

It is vitally important that we recognize our need for prayer. Jesus said that men ought always to pray, and not to lose heart (Luke 18:1). We should pray without ceasing (1 Thess. 5:17). Prayer is how we connect Heaven to Earth! We don't pray "just because." We pray in hopes of an answer. We pray because we recognize our finite state of existence, knowing we don't have the power to bring about the desired result of a petitioned prayer. We look to the One who we know has the power to change our situation. We recognize our *need* for prayer. Not only do we need prayers of petition, but again, we need prayer to reconnect with God, to recognize His sovereignty, power, authority, omniscience, etc.

Prayer is usually birthed out of need. But oftentimes we go through life with a sense of self-sufficiency. We pray — but we often do so in desperate times, not mixing it with faith. However, I believe people turn to prayer as a "last resort" because, deep down inside, we know that we "need" to pray. It's innate. Even people who don't have a relationship with God tend to resort to prayer in desperate times. Deep inside they realize that what they're asking for is beyond their ability to "fix." So, they pray.

There will never be prayer, effective or otherwise, without the realization that God is the Source for the answer to the issues you face. Recognize that you can't call yourself a Believer and yet remain slack in prayer as though it is not a need. You must realize your need for prayer. Don't wait until "life happens" to you – when obstacles come your way and you finally give things over to God. Realize that you need God in everything and that you must stay in constant fellowship with Him. And the way you do that is to pray and spend time with the Lord. Just as you must talk with people on a regular basis to stay connected, you must spend time talking with God, to keep that Divine Connection to the Source intact.

When you recognize your need for God and that the way you connect with Him is through prayer, then you will recognize your *need* for prayer; and God will begin answering because you now believe prayer works and He's your Source for the answer.

Live Out Loud

Prayer:

*Today, Lord, I recognize my **need** for prayer. I can do nothing worthwhile by my own works. But with you I can do all things and nothing is impossible to me. I humble myself, Lord, so that in prayer my finite being (the Enos in me) can connect with Your infinite, tapping into the eternal and bringing it into my present. In Jesus Name, Amen!*

Action:

Faith without works is dead. Take some quiet time to get alone with God and focus on your need for prayer and to improve your prayer life.

Psalm 65:2, NIV > *"O You who hear prayer, To You all people will come."*

List 3 things you intend to pray about, now that you
understand your need for prayer:

1. _____

2. _____

3. _____

Write down your "take-a-ways" from this lesson on
Recognize Your Need for Prayer:

_____

_____

_____

_____

_____

Prayer does not equip us for greater works — prayer is the greater work.

– Oswald Chambers

And Satan trembles when he sees, the weakest saint upon his knees.

– William Cowper

CHAPTER 3

Recognize The Value of Prayer

. . . for mine house shall be called a house of prayer for all people. (Isaiah 56:7, KJV)

You may be wondering exactly how important our prayers are to God? I mean, let's be honest, not all prayers get answered. I hear people all the time say that God says "yes, no, or maybe." I don't remember seeing that anywhere in scripture so I tend toward believing God for the "yes." 2 Corinthians 1:20 says that "all the *promises* of God find their 'Yes' in Him." If we pray according to His Word He always says yes bc it's His Word and it does what He sends it to do (Isaiah 55:10-11). If we are asking for things that aren't the will of God for our lives they won't get answered anyway.

Now, let me pause for a minute here. I know what you're thinking. If we know it's God's will to heal then why are some not healed? Obviously, I can't answer that. I, myself, have things in my life that have happened and I don't understand why God hasn't answered that prayer, or prayers. I know it's His will but I haven't seen it happen yet.

Katherine Kuhlman and Smith Wiggleworth wondered the same thing. They both said that would be the first thing they asked when they got to heaven, "Why wasn't everyone healed?" Only God knows the answer to that question. My husband says that everyone gets healed, we just don't see it because it happened when they died and entered eternity. That's one way to look at it. Personally, I believe that in many instances it has to do with faith in some way. It could be the faith of the one needing the prayer answered, the faith of those who are praying with and for that person, or even the level of faith within an atmosphere. We see all of these examples in scripture. Jesus said to some, "Your faith has made you whole." To others he healed because of the faith of their friends or the faith of someone in authority (like the centurion or a parent). And yet, it is mentioned that Jesus didn't heal much in his hometown because of unbelief. I believe in that situation that it was perhaps an "atmospheric" lack of faith, so to speak. Regardless of why people don't receive an answer to prayer, especially prayers of healing, we know that the "reason" is not because God is somehow at fault. He desires to "not withhold any good thing" from those who walk uprightly and are His children (Luke 12:32; Ps. 84:11).

Since God already knows the plans He has for us and the outcome for each prayer we pray, then how valuable are our prayers? We may need to pray in order to commune with

God but does He really consider our requests valid or valuable?

First, let's look at Isaiah 56:7. God said His "house" will be called "a house of prayer for all people." Now, we know He's talking about a place where He resides. In the old testament His presence rested on the mercy seat of the arc of the covenant within the tent, then within the temple. But in the New Testament our bodies are referred to as the temple of the Holy Spirit. The Holy Spirit has come to "dwell" on the inside of believers and followers of Jesus Christ. We are now the house where God dwells.

So, let's start at a very basic understanding of what a house is. A house is a dwelling place – a place for someone to live, abide, or in which to take up residence. 1 Corinthians 6:19a (NASB) says *"Or do you not know that your body is a temple* [house] *of the Holy Spirit within you, whom you have from God? . . .'* And again in 1 Corinthians 3:16 (NASB), *'Do you not know that you are God's temple and that God's Spirit dwells in you?"* We see here that *we* are the temple, (i.e. house) of the Holy Spirit. We are His dwelling place; the place where He lives and has taken up residence. This, of course, is only possible if we have received the Spirit which comes at the point of salvation. God, then, dwells in us. We are His house! So, when we read in Isaiah 56:7 that God's house is a house of prayer, we understand that we don't just *do* prayer, we *are* prayer. His house, His dwelling place, which is us, is to be a house of prayer. We shouldn't just pray *some*times; our whole being should be prayer. Prayer is the dwelling place of God! It's His house! God's house isn't made of natural materials like wood, brick, or stone. It's not made with hands (Acts 7:48; 17:24b). His house is made of prayer (1 Pe. 2:5).

Just as a natural house must have a foundation on which to build, so do we. Jesus is that Rock. He's a "sure foundation" and the cornerstone of God's house (Eph. 2:20). He secures the building. Believers are like the materials (the Word says that we are lively stones – 1 Pe. 2:5). And prayer is like the mortar. It is the thing that unites the building to its foundation. Prayer keeps the building stable, strong, and enduring — individually and corporately. Just like mortar is invaluable to the construction of a good, solid house, so prayer is invaluable to us, holding us together, keeping us connected, stone to stone, and to the chief cornerstone. Prayer helps us resist the storms that come. Prayer makes us that spiritual house, offering up spiritual sacrifices (1 Pe. 2:5).

It's worth repeating . . . the Spirit of God lives in us and we are, to Him, called the place of prayer. We should not just involve ourselves with the *act* of praying. We should *live* prayer. That is how we pray without ceasing (1 Thess. 5:17). Prayer is so valuable to our lives, not just to receive something from God but to be able to hear Him more clearly, knowing His voice and the direction of the Spirit. This is done through fellowshipping with Him in prayer.

Can you now see how valuable prayer is to our relationship with God?

Let's look a little further. There's more value to be found in prayer. Rev. 5:8 says, "*And when he had taken the scroll, the four living creatures and the twenty-four elders fell down before the Lamb, each holding a harp, and golden bowls full of incense, which are the prayers of the saints.*""*And another angel came and stood at the altar with a golden censer, and he was given much incense to offer with the prayers of all the saints on the golden altar before the throne,*" (Rev. 8:3). These scriptures are powerful! They tell us that prayer is precious and like a fragrance to God. Prayers are so valuable that He keeps them in golden bowls! I thought about one translation that says "vials." A vial is what we use today to hold medicine. So, looking at it like this we see that God places our prayers in golden containers that will heal, deliver, and soothe the soul (just thought I'd bring a little prophetic revelation to the text). But we can see here in Revelations that God doesn't trash our prayers or stuff them in a box. He doesn't listen to them haphazardly or consider them insignificant. He seals them in *gold* until He is ready to release them into the atmosphere. They are precious and priceless to Him. Wow! Isn't that awesome? Reading that just gets me even more excited about prayer, knowing how valuable they are to the Lord. And we should place the same value on prayer as God does! They should be like gold to us. Do you throw up prayers recklessly? Or do you pray with the understanding that they are going up to God fragranted and wrapped in gold?

Obviously, we are now realizing that prayer is extremely important to God. Before we can pray effectively (i.e. prayer that yields its intended result) we must recognize its value and understand the magnitude of its limitless possibilities! Prayer is where God lives! Do you want to live where God lives? Pray. Do you want God's presence? Pray. Do you want to know His will? Pray. Do you want to be the house that God built? Pray. Pray. Pray. God "dwells in tents not made with hands." He lives in us. We are His house. And we are called "a house of prayer."

Prayer is our means of communication and fellowship with God. Just like our phone is a lifeline in times of crisis, prayer is our lifeline . . . *period*! Every answer is indeed only a prayer away.

Lastly, in understanding the value of prayer, let me make it clear that prayer outside of its intended purpose or offered to an "unknown god," won't work. We can't pray to a false god and expect anything just because we "prayed." As we now better understand prayer, we know that there is only one God with whom we commune and to whom we offer up prayers. We must pray to the only One who can answer our prayer and pray according to His Word, upholding the truths and principles of His Word. Begin today to place a higher value on prayer and watch God move mountains in your life!

Live Out Loud

Prayer:

Lord, I profess to value prayer from this day on. Because I value it, I will determine to be continually prayerful. I will consider what I am praying, pray from my heart, and stay mindful of how much my prayers mean to You. Amen.

Action:

Think of ways you can be "continually" prayerful and write them down.

1 Sam. 12:23, NKJV > *Moreover, as for me, God forbid that I should sin against the Lord in ceasing to pray for you . . .*

Luke 18:1b, NKJV > *. . . that men ought always to pray, and not to faint.*

List 3 things about your prayer life that you can change to show that you value prayer:

1. _____

2. _____

3. _____

Write down your "take-a-ways" from this lesson on Recognizing the Value of Prayer:

_____

_____

_____

_____

_____

Holiness is the architectural plan on which God buildeth up his living temple.

– Charles Spurgeon

It must be a prospect pleasing to God to see His creatures forever drawing nearer to Him by greater degrees of resemblance.

– Joseph Addison

CHAPTER 4

Pray in Righteousness

*The effectual fervent prayer of a **righteous** man avails much (James 5:16b, NKJV)*

This verse is filled with ways to make our prayers effective. Before we deal with each one let's briefly discuss what it means to "avail much." The Greek word here is *ischuo*, meaning "to be strong, or have power." Its usage means "I have strength, am strong, am in full health and vigor, am able; I prevail" [Strong's Greek: 2480 (*isxýō*)]. Properly, it means "embodied strength that [*engages*] the resistance. For the believer, *"avail much"*, refers to the Lord strengthening us with *combative, confrontive* force to achieve all He gives faith for. That is, *facing necessary resistance* that brings what the *Lord* defines is success (*His* victory). These are the kind of prayers we want to pray. Prayers that have power and prevail. Prayers that are filled with a confrontive force that brings victory in the face of resistance. And these types of prayers are effectual and fervent and imminent from a person who is in right standing with God. We will deal with each aspect of this type of prayer person over the next few chapters.

James 5:16b tells us that this person is a *righteous person.* According to God's Word, righteous people can accomplish a lot through prayer. But what exactly does it mean to be righteous? The word righteousness as defined by Webster's Dictionary is "the conformity of heart and life to divine law, or purity of heart and rectitude of life. It is also defined as just, equitable, or merited. When applied to people, righteousness means being holy in heart and observant of divine commands." In this passage the Greek word, *dikaiou,* means "righteous, observing divine and human laws; one who is such as he ought to be; in a wide sense, upright, righteous, virtuous, keeping the commands of God."

When discussing righteousness most Christians simply state, "I am the righteousness of Christ." While that is certainly true according to God's Word, it somehow seems to take the responsibility of righteousness (i.e. right standing with God; right living) completely off us. The need for teaching on righteousness in the lives of Believers is often neglected, or not enforced, from the pulpit. Sure, we have preachers who try to "force feed" holiness into people but I'm talking about teaching messages that convict the hearts of Believers to want to continuously live in right standing with God.

Let's revisit the righteousness of Christ for a moment. Christ lived free from sin and in the perfect will of God. He was in "right standing" with God. He was/is Righteousness! Through His death and subsequent resurrection His righteousness was imputed to us. When we believe on Him and receive Him as Savior, we now have "right standing" with God. This does not, however, remove the responsibility *we* have to live clean, godly lives. Actually, it's because of what Christ did for us that should compel us to follow His example in holy living.

As a matter of fact, and truth, God sent the Holy Spirit to convict the world of sin and to comfort and guide the Believer into all truth. He helps us live holy. God said, "Be holy, for I am Holy." We aren't just supposed to go through life with an "oops, God forgive me I'm only human" mentality. We sound like that secular song that says, "I'm only human after all, don't put the blame on me." Actually, if we are born AGAIN we are no longer "just human." Jesus was both fully human and fully God (Colossians 2:9). If we are filled with God's Spirit, are we not then also fully human and fully god? God has come to live inside those who believe. We are no longer "only human." We have been filled with His Spirit and are to *pursue* righteousness (1 Tim. 6:11; 2 Ti. 2:22).

If you find difficulty in praying or getting answers to prayer, try repenting of both known and unknown sin. Ask the Holy Spirit to reveal any sin to you, whether committed or omitted, so that you can confess it and turn from it. Unconfessed sins are a huge barrier to effective prayer. Jesus died for our "sin." That is to say, the sin nature. We have been delivered from the *penalty* of sin, or the sin nature. We now, however, are responsible for living according to our *new* nature and to deal with the *power* of sin by yielding our bodies as a living sacrifice (Rom. 12:1). We may be tempted to revert back to our old nature and commit "acts of sin." Jesus died for our sin nature, so salvation takes place only once. But if we give in to the desires of the flesh and commit an act of sin we must still repent. To repent does not mean to simply be sorry for or regretful about something we've done, said, or thought. It means to change our mind, to turn and go in the other direction.

Keep yourself unspotted from the world. Confess your sins to God. Remember to ask the Holy Spirit to "create in me [you] a clean heart, O God, and renew a <u>right</u> spirit within me [you]" (Ps. 51:10). Prayer will become so much easier after repentance has taken place.

Live Out Loud

Prayer:

Lord, I thank you that I am the righteousness of Christ. Jesus, thank You for what You did to cover my sin with Your love and fill me with righteousness by Your Spirit. Now, Lord, help me to live righteous. I determine today, God, to consecrate myself more completely to You. I will endeavor to live holy, because You are Holy. I repent (change my mind and turn in the other direction) from

I trust in your strength to keep me in righteousness. Purify me, Lord, from the inside out. In Jesus Name. Amen.

Ps. 34:15 > *The eyes of the Lord are toward the righteous, and His ears toward their cry.*

Action:

Take some time to think about your daily life. Is there anything that you feel hinders or contaminates your spirit? It can be TV, Music, bad relationships, etc. Make a decision to abstain from this for a day, week, or longer and see how you feel spiritually.

Proverbs 12:26 > *The righteous is a guide to his neighbor, But the way of the wicked leads them astray.*

Romans 12:2 > *And do not be conformed to this world, but be transformed by the renewing of your mind, so that you may prove what the will of God is, that which is good and acceptable and perfect.*

List 3 things you're asking God to help you overcome:

1. _____

2. _____

3. _____

Write down your "take-a-ways" from this lesson on Pray in Righteousness:

_____

_____

_____

_____

_____

Never be lacking in zeal, but keep your spiritual fervor, serving the Lord.

– Romans 12:11, NIV

Wesley was once asked how he got the crowds. He replied, "I set myself on fire, and the people came to see me burn."

– Maxwell Droke

CHAPTER 5

Pray with Passion

The . . . fervent prayer. . . avails much (James 5:16)

This same text (as discussed in chapter 4) has so much insight and detail into prayer that each part deserves its own chapter. The focus in this chapter is the part of the text where James refers to effective prayers as those that are done with fervency. What does it mean to pray fervently? Why is that important? How do we do that?

To pray fervently means to pray with an intense, passionate spirit. It means to pray with enthusiasm. Be excited that you are entering into a time alone with God. If two people are in love and getting ready to go on a date, they get excited. Why? Because they get to spend some quality face to face time with the one they adore. They get to share their experiences and their desires; and they get to learn more about the other person. Passion and excitement can encourage and inspire, as well as garner the attention of the other person.

This is how we should be in our prayer time with the Lord. We should be excited about sharing our heart and learning more about Him. We can pray with excitement and listen for God's passionate response.

Jesus said that in the latter days the hearts of many will grow cold (Mt. 24:12b). While this text isn't referring to a new Believer in particular, I thought about how many Christians "cool off" shortly after their initial conversion experience. Their heart no longer melts with compassion or pants after God. The seed of His Word is permitted to plant and germinate, but their roots are shallow and the Word ends up having been planted on stony ground. Stony ground is "fallow" ground. This is a ground that is hard and stubborn. It is full of rocks and must be "broken" up before planting can take root. The Word says that affliction or persecution comes "and they are offended". Offense hardens the heart and reduces the flame of passion. "The seed becomes a weed." A new believer may get offended by "Christians not acting like Christians." Or, maybe they don't like that the Word reveals their shortcomings. Or sometimes they're just tired of "defending their faith," albeit short-lived, and simply find it easier to be like the world than face persecution or affliction. But Jesus said that offenses must come and that the one offending will face judgment. Don't let the "god of this world" cause you to live in the spirit of offense. Let the truth of God's Word take root on the inside of you. Break up your fallow ground through repentance and humility.

A lack of fervency is perhaps one of the biggest detriments to the success of the Body of Christ. It is our "blessed hope" and the "joy set before us" that should stir our hearts to become passionate about the things of God. Fervency is often diminished because "gladness [joy] has dried up" (Joel 1:12). When we lose (or misplace) the joy of our salvation we often lose the fervency, or passion, in our prayer life. I have studied joy and how we lose it and how we can restore it back to our lives. That's another book, but I will share one of the ways to help restore joy . . . it is to read the Word of God. Jeremiah said that he ate of God's Word and it became his joy (Jer. 15:16). There's no better place to begin the journey back to joy-filled living than to read and meditate on God's Word. Also, remember that joy is a fruit of the spirit. If we are walking in the spirit, we should be emanating joy. Joy can help restore, or create, a passionate prayer life.

Joy, passion, and fervency are all forms of zeal. The Bible says, "the zeal of Your house has consumed me" (Ps. 69:9; Jn. 2:17). We should be consumed with zeal, fervency for God's house. Remember, God's house is a house of prayer. Like Jesus, we should allow the zealousness of prayer to "eat us up." We should be filled with a zeal for God's house – "eat up" with a zeal for prayer! Consumed with a passion and desire to meet with God! Overtaken with fervency! We should be so filled with a zealousness for prayer that others will see it and remark that "he/she is eat up with it (zeal)."

So, how do we become fervent and passionate in our prayers? Glad you asked. Here are a few things you can do to become zealous about prayer. Along with increasing your joy, you should:

1. **Confess any sin** – We discussed this earlier but it bears repeating. We are not to operate in condemnation but should take note of areas in our life where we may be catering to the desires of the flesh rather than the things of the Spirit. Prayer is a spiritual activity. We cannot bring our flesh into a spiritual place. One of the ways we can ensure that is to confess any known sin. Remember also not to be in a place of offense. We can sometimes be offended and not even know it. Offense and other things can lead to unforgiveness, bitterness, or resentment. These are HUGE barriers to answered prayer and we should deal with them before we enter into deeper prayer. These things are very subtle and the enemy will use them against you if you are not watchful and quick to repent.

2. **Be sure to read Gods' Word daily** – If we allow it, God's Word will begin to soften any hardened areas in your heart and life. There is nothing more powerful than God's Word! He has the "words of life" and your life here on earth is lived out more

fully as you read, study, absorb, and live out the Word of God. His Word can help you with prayer in general and with inspiring passionate prayer. When we understand that God is bound by His Word to perform it then we can be assured that our prayers will be answered when we pray His Word. We can only do that if we are familiar with the Word by reading and studying it. This helps build our confidence in prayer, which creates passion in our pursuit.

3. **Surround yourself with passionate people** – There's a saying that "love is contagious." Passion can be contagious too. Have you ever been around someone who got so excited about something that you got excited too? You may not have even known what they were excited about yet but you find yourself moving in that direction. It's important to surround yourself with people who are excited about the things of God, especially those who are excited about prayer. One of the inspirations for revising this prayer book came through Terri Copeland Pearsons. As I was watching a Believer's Convention I listened as she taught on prayer. She is so excited about prayer that it inspired me to add more to this book. I have been to pre-service prayer, but most are either too dull or too "over the top " without the richness of authentic prayer. But she was/is passionate about

prayer and I wish I could have been in person, even if only for the pre-service prayer. It's important to get around passionate praying Believers; not those who seem superficially excited but who are, instead, genuinely filled with joy and have a passion for God's presence. It *can* be contagious.

4. **Pray in the Spirit often** – Paul told Timothy to "stir up the gift." I deal with this a little more in chapter 8. But praying in the Spirit is a wonderful opportunity to encourage yourself to become more passionate in prayer. The Spirit "builds up." It edifies us when we avail ourselves to pray this way. I discuss this in more detail in Chapter 8.

5. **Think on God's promises, on Heaven, etc.** – Keep your mind on good and pleasant things. We are bombarded daily with bad news and evil all around. Setting our minds on things above and not on the things of this world helps keep our focus and refreshes us with a passionate heart for God and His presence.

6. **Focus on the needs of others** – Setting our heart and mind on doing the will of God by showing compassion for others can help us by getting our minds off of our own issues and allowing the hurts and pains of others to penetrate our heart and create a zeal for action. Think of a mission or personal interest for which you can pray. If you are passionate

about helping the homeless, for example, begin to pray for those in your area. Fervent prayer should come easy when we pray for those we are passionate to help.

7. **Ask God to rekindle your flame!** – enough said here really! But we can ask the Lord to create a hunger and thirst for a passionate prayer life and know that we will be filled.

Live Out Loud

Prayer:

Lord, create in me a fire, a passion for prayer. Your house is a house of prayer and just as Jesus had a zeal for your house, for prayer, give me an enthusiastic desire to pray.

Action:

Take a moment and follow the steps above and leap into a time of passionate prayer. You may not "feel it" yet, but keep trying daily and watch God fill you with passion. If you need help getting the embers to catch fire, try thinking about someone, or a people group, that you feel very passionate about helping.

(One of the ways I create passion in my prayer time is to listen to passionate music. I used to have a worship CD that also had prayer and prophetic exhortation in it. It was a powerful tool to help me pray with passion).

1 Chr. 16:11 > *Seek the Lord and His strength, seek His face continually.*

List 3 spiritual actions that can bring out your passion (like music, the Word, an underserved population, etc.):

1. _____

2. _____

3. _____

Write down your "take-a-ways" from this lesson on Pray with Passion:

_____

_____

_____

_____

_____

The one who calls you is faithful, and He will do it.

– 1 Thessalonians 5:24

If you don't have confidence, you'll always find a way not to win.

– Carl Lewis

CHAPTER 6

Pray with Meaningful Intent

The . . . effectual prayers . . . avail much (James 5:16, KJV)

Continuing our insight with the book of James, chapter 5, verse 16, we find that the "effectual" prayers also accomplish much. The Greek word here for effectual is *energeo* (where we get the word, energy). It means to be "active," "mighty in," effectual, even fervent. But it would be redundant for James to simply repeat the word fervent. Webster's dictionary defines effectual as "producing an intended effect; valid or binding, as an agreement or document; something (i.e. *prayer*) that produces a decisive outcome or result." In other words, we should pray with meaningful intent and with a specific result in mind. Not random, meaningless prayers.

Pray, not only with passion, but also with assured-ness that the answer will be just as you have prayed. Pray with the understanding that prayer *does* work. Pray with a focus. Pray – knowing God's covenant agreement with you.

Don't pray useless, wasteful prayers or with inability. Don't just pray mindless and empty repetitious prayers like the heathen (Mt. 6:7). Pray in confidence, with full intent – wholly understanding and acknowledging your privilege and right to pray, due to the blood of Jesus.

The best example of an effectual prayer is at the resurrection of Lazarus. Jesus prayed to the Father saying, "Father, I thank You that You have heard me. And I know that You hear me always." Then He spoke to Lazarus, and Lazarus rose from the dead. He was confident that God would hear His prayer and answer according to His faith!

The prayers of Jesus were never without purpose. Our prayers sometimes may seem "hopeless," when, in actuality, they're just purposeless. God isn't a random God. He has a plan and a purpose for everything He does and says. Don't shout out prayers like an aimless arrow. If you had a bow and arrow and a target in front of you, would you shoot the arrow aimlessly and still hope it hits the target? Of course not. With great intent and purpose you would shoot the arrow as perfectly as possible toward its intended target; and you would believe that it's possible to hit it before even releasing the arrow. Apply the same intent, purpose, and faith to your prayers.

When you pray, do you pray with an end result in mind? Do you pray intentionally and with purpose? Or, are your prayers often empty and without meaning or depth? Are they random and aimless, not expecting to hit the target? I've had many prayers like this. We can often fall into habitual prayers. We might say something like, "I pray for . . . well, you know God." Or, we don't direct our prayers towards any specific thing. Even today's experts tell us that when setting S.M.A.R.T. goals the first thing is to BE SPECIFIC! "Shoot for the moon. Even if you miss it you will land among the stars."

Prayers must come from the heart, not the head. When you pray for a great day, do you really have confidence that the day will be great? Are you praying intentionally?

This is the substance of an effectual prayer. Those who pray with effect, expect results! They believe that God will answer, that He will honor His promises, and that their prayers "avail much" (greatly prosper; have effect or advantage). That's why it's important to know the promises and will of God. When we *know* it's His will to heal, then we can be assured, or certain, that our prayer will be answered. Sometimes we just have to wait in faith, believing. It may not happen according to our timing, but it will happen. Even if it's upon our entering eternity. But we still remain steadfast in our prayers, no matter what it looks like. We don't pray "if it's your will" because His Word *is* His will. "And this is the confidence that we have toward Him, that if we ask anything according to His will He hears us" (1 John 5:14). We pray in confidence. If the prayer doesn't get answered like we believed then we just have to trust God and know that He is not at fault. We know in part . . . and even when the prayers don't get answered or don't get answered in the time we thought they should, we usually learn great life lessons from the experience. God's purposes will prevail.

So, make sure your prayers are intentional. I sometimes use "declarations" in my prayer time to help me harness the Truth of God's Word plus the power of intentionality. For example, I will take a scripture like 2 Corinthians 9:7-8 (NIV), which says, *"Each one should give what he has decided in his heart to give, not out of regret or compulsion. For God loves a cheerful giver.And God is able to make all grace abound to you, so that in all things, at all times, having all that you need, you will abound in every good work,* and I will declare that "I give I am a giver! I love to give! I have plenty of money to give away all the time and I live in abundance!"

Our prayers must have a significant purpose. We must believe that we will receive. Hebrews 11:1 (KJV) says that "Now faith is the substance of things hoped for, the evidence of things not seen." The word hope in this text means *expectation.* We *expect* our faith to produce what we say. EXPECTING our prayers to be answered accordingly is praying with meaningful intent, an "effectual" prayer.

Live Out Loud

Prayer:

Today, Lord, I am making a commitment to start praying with meaningful intent, expecting that my prayers will bring about the desired end, according to your Word and your will. I will not pray shallow, empty prayers. I will pray in confidence, expecting to receive the fruit of my prayers.

Action:

Choose something, or someone, to pray for or about. Make it specific but keep it simple. Build your faith up to believe for the answer before you pray. Then, pray what you've learned (chapters 1-6) and believe that the answer will be just as you asked. Make sure it is something according to God's Word. Give it time . . . keep believing.

Hebrews 3:6, NKJV > *But Christ as a son over His own house, whose house we are if we hold fast the confidence and the rejoicing of the hope firm to the end.*

List 3 prayers that you're *expecting* God to answer for you:

1. _____

2. _____

3. _____

Write down your "take-a-ways" from this lesson on Pray with Fervency (Meaningful Intent):

_____

_____

_____

_____

_____

If you don't have faith, pray anyway. If you don't understand or believe the words you're saying, pray anyway. Prayer can start faith, particularly if you pray aloud. And even the most imperfect prayer is an attempt to reach God.

– Cary Grant

So Jesus said to them, "Because of your unbelief; for assuredly, I say to you, if you have faith as a mustard seed, you will say to this mountain, 'Move from here to there,' and it will move; and nothing will be impossible for you.

– Matthew 17:20

CHAPTER 7

Pray in Faith

"Therefore I tell you, whatever you ask in prayer, believe that you have received it, and it will be yours." (Mark 11:24)

"And whatever you ask in prayer, you will receive, if you have faith." (Mt. 21:22)

This is probably the most important element of answered prayer! God has designed His entire Kingdom to operate by FAITH! It is by faith that we're saved! So, it would only make sense that every promise to be received must be done so by faith.

Hebrews 11:1 (KJV) says that "faith is the substance of things hoped for, the evidence of things not seen." Though many people, when they speak of hope, usually imply some uncertainty or doubt, that is not an accurate understanding. As discussed in a previous chapter, whenever hope is mentioned in the Bible it actually means *expectation*. It is not some *wishful* thinking as though it might not actually happen. It is *expected* to happen! We do not wonder if God will answer, we expect Him to do so. Since hope means expectation, we can say that faith is the *substance* of things *expected* and the evidence of things not seen. God answers to the *expectation* that is *substantiated* by our faith, not a hope that consists of doubt.Faith, then, involves trusting in God's promises even when we cannot physically see the outcome.

Faith should be the substance of our expectations; the thing that brings to pass what we are asking and/or expecting. Praying "in faith" is the evidence that your prayers are, or will, be answered.

Sometimes, we purchase items we don't yet have in our possession but we have a receipt for them. That receipt is our *evidence*, our assurance that we will have those things we requested. Faith is the trust we put in the company and postal service to deliver what we requested and paid for. Faith, though intangible, manifests tangible things. Jesus already paid for every request you will make! There's no better receipt of faith.

He said when you pray, believe you've already received them (your requests) and you will have them. Faith (belief) is the evidence (receipt). Faith is what God answers to. "Without faith, it is impossible to please God" (Hebrews 11:6, NIV). Jesus paid it all, and your faith is proof (the receipt for it). Faith is the very essence of the request.

Without it, our prayers are to no avail. They do not, and will not, prosper.

Faith is fundamentally foundational to our belief system as Christians. We must believe that He is! The Word says that we can *speak* things into existence by faith, we can *believe* for God's promises by faith, but we must also *pray in* faith. When you make a request unto God, believe that He hears you and will answer. Have faith that what you're asking will surely come to pass. Don't pray "hoping" – pray EXPECTING!

A very prominent minister of faith by the name of Smith Wigglesworth once said that "our prayers are in vain unless we really expect what we ask to be granted to us . . . and if you have prayed for something 5 times, the first 4 weren't in faith." Wow! The latter part of this quote has caused me to pray more fervently and in greater faith. I've learned to pray for something once and wait on the Lord to answer, believing, like Jesus, that He hears me always. This is not to say that I've never asked again, more than once, for something. But I remind myself it's already done and start thanking God in advance for the answer.

Though I touch on some of the following points in other chapters, let me list here 5 truths from the Word of God that will hopefully help you pray in faith:

1. Pray with Boldness and Confidence: When we pray in faith, we approach God with boldness and

confidence, believing that He hears and answers our prayers according to His will:

- "Therefore let us approach the throne of grace with boldness, so that we may receive mercy and find grace to help us in time of need." (Hebrews 4:16)

- "This is the confidence we have in approaching God: that if we ask anything according to his will, he hears us." (1 John 5:14)

2. Pray Persistently and with Perseverance: Praying in faith involves persistence and perseverance, trusting that God will answer our prayers in His perfect timing. Being persistent doesn't have to mean that we lacked faith the first time we asked. We can remind God of His Word and that we're standing in agreement with His Word.

- "Ask and it will be given to you; seek and you will find; knock and the door will be opened to you." (Matthew 7:7)

- "Be joyful in hope, patient in affliction, faithful in prayer." (Romans 12:12)

3. Pray with Thanksgiving: In our prayers of faith, we express gratitude to God for His past faithfulness and anticipate His continued provision and blessings.

- "Do not be anxious about anything, but in every situation, by prayer and petition, with thanksgiving, present your requests to God." (Philippians 4:6)

- "Give thanks in all circumstances; for this is God's will for you in Christ Jesus." (1 Thessalonians 5:18)

4. Pray According to God's Will: I dive into God's will in a later chapter, but let me briefly state that praying in faith involves aligning our prayers with God's will, trusting that His plans are ultimately for our good and His glory.

- "This is the confidence we have in approaching God: that if we ask anything according to his will, he hears us." (1 John 5:14)

- "Your kingdom come, your will be done, on earth as it is in heaven." (Matthew 6:10)

5. Pray Expectantly and with Faith-Filled Belief: Praying in faith requires expecting God to act and believing that He is able to do far more abundantly than all we ask or imagine.

- "Therefore I tell you, whatever you ask for in prayer, believe that you have received it, and it will be yours." (Mark 11:24)

- "Now to him who is able to do immeasurably more than all we ask or imagine, according to his power that is at work within us." (Ephesians 3:20)

Praying in faith involves approaching God with boldness, persistence, and thanksgiving, aligning our prayers with His will, and believing expectantly in His power to answer according to His wisdom and love.

Live Out Loud

Prayer:

Lord, I believe. Help my unbelief. Use your Word, Lord, to increase my faith because I know that when I pray in faith, believing, and not doubting in my heart, I will have what I request. Amen

Action:

"Faith comes by 'hearing'" implies not only the physical act of hearing the message but also the understanding and acceptance of its content. So, in the context of Romans 10:17, "hearing" encompasses both the reception of the message through the ears and the comprehension or understanding of its meaning. Find some scriptures about faith, or a particular need, and read them. Then, begin meditating on the study and push that seed of truth deeper into your spirit. Start saying the scriptures out loud (make them personal). You will feel yourself begin to believe them more and more. Then, pray the prayer of faith.

Hebrews 11:6 > *"And without faith it is impossible to please Him [God], for whoever would draw near to God must believe that He exists and that He rewards those who seek Him. "*.

List 3 scriptures that support your prayer requests (write them out in personal form):

1. _____

2. _____

3. _____

Write down your "take-a-ways" from this lesson on Pray in Faith:

_____

_____

_____

_____

_____

Groanings which cannot be uttered are often prayers which cannot be refused.

– Charles Spurgeon

. . . Not by might, nor by power, but by my Spirit, says the Lord Almighty.

– Zechariah 4:6 (TLB)

CHAPTER 8

Pray in the Spirit

"Likewise the Spirit helps us in our weakness. For we do not know what to pray for as we ought, but the Spirit himself intercedes for us with groanings too deep for words. And he who searches hearts knows what is the mind of the Spirit, because the Spirit intercedes for the saints according to the will of God." (Romans 8:26-27)

Extremely important, and perhaps second to faith with regards to prayer, is praying in the Spirit. I'm not sure why praying in the Spirit is not often a focus in many churches. In some circles of the Christian faith it's neglected, unheard of, and even shunned or scorned. But if we want to be truly effective in prayer it is a wonderful privilege to pray this way. Do we not desire to know the will of God? Do we, as Believers, not also desire to DO the will of God? But there are times when we simply don't know what to pray for, or *how* to pray. If we pray in the Spirit, however, He intercedes on our behalf according to the will of God. They are One and God knows the mind of the Spirit (Romans 8:27).

Praying in the Spirit *is* praying the will of God with the expectation that God will answer our prayer. If it's His will, He'll do it. Right? Actually, this is probably the best way to pray if you want to ensure your prayers get answered. Jude 20 tells us that our "most holy faith" takes place when we pray in the Holy Ghost (i.e. in the Spirit). It doesn't say that praying in the Spirit is simply praying "in faith," or in "holy faith." It says that it's our MOST holy faith. When we pray in the Spirit, it is our greatest, purest form of faith. When faith is perfect, it cannot fail. It is guaranteed!

Romans 8:26a says the Spirit helps our weaknesses (our physical weakness, frailty, or character defect) because we don't know what we should pray for "as we ought." First, let me make note of the fact that we *should* know what to pray for. The word *ought* is the same as "ought to," or "should." We *should* know. I mean, we can look at the world, our nation, our families, our own personal struggles and see many things to which we could direct our prayers. However, we obviously often fall short of knowing what to pray for; thus, the Holy Spirit steps in and intercedes on our behalf (if we allow Him to, of course). Romans 8:26b says "with groanings too deep for words." The Spirit groans in us. Have you ever experienced a time where words couldn't express what was going on inside of you? Tears can express happiness, pain, or heartache; laughter is an expression of joy; moaning is an expression of anguish or grief; screaming can signify joy, anger, or used as a "release" for frustration. Groanings in prayer are an expression of the Spirit praying *through* us. If you want your prayers answered, you don't always have to know what to pray for, or how to pray . . . just pray in the Spirit and the will of God shall be done.

Ephesians 6:18a says to "pray at all times in the Spirit!" This is not written in the form of a suggestion. This entire passage about putting on the armor of God and the mention of praying at all times in the Spirit is written in the "imperative, active" voice. When something is written in the imperative, active voice, it means that the sentence is structured to give a direct command or instruction, and the subject of the sentence is performing the action. This style of writing is often used to convey a sense of urgency, clarity, and directness in communication.

For example, in the sentence "Close the door," the verb "close" is in the imperative form, giving a command, and the subject "you" (though not explicitly stated) is performing the action of closing the door. This creates a straightforward and commanding tone. In essence, imperative, active voice writing tells the reader what to do and puts the emphasis on action. So, we can understand clearly here that as Believers we should actively participate in praying in the Spirit.

To further explain, this is not a little "s" spirit as some may teach. It is not our spirit praying. It is the Holy Spirit praying through us. Paul said he prays with understanding, but also in the Spirit (capital "S"). And in the discussion in 1 Corinthians, chapters 14 & 15 Paul is referring to praying in the Spirit as "praying in tongues."

We should seek God on what to pray for and pray with an understanding of what we're saying (especially in the company of others who may not understand "praying in the Spirit"). And when we don't know what to pray for, we should pray in the Spirit (i.e. pray in tongues). We should allow the Spirit to fill us to overflow until we utter the language of "angels" as Paul says. At the very least, we should pray with "groanings" that are too deep for words.

Unfortunately, the Church has downplayed praying in the Spirit because of 1 Cor. 14 & 15, and because of the divisiveness of discussion on tongues and the Baptism of the Holy Spirit. But the Word is still true today. Praying in the Spirit gets results. Many can attest to this fact. I thoroughly enjoy praying in tongues. It edifies my spirit and I know, based on the Word, that it is my most holy faith and the will of God that is being spoken. In addition, praying in the Spirit edifies us and "builds us up" (Jude 1:20). My mind doesn't have to understand the words to know that my prayers are heard and WILL come to pass.

Live Out Loud

Prayer:

Thank you, Lord, for the precious gift of the Holy Spirit. Lord, fill me today with your Spirit. Let it overflow with power; let it edify my soul and spirit. I surrender and am ready to receive. In Jesus' Name, Amen.

Action:

If you've never spoken in the prayer language, (i.e. in tongues) take a moment alone in your prayer time and ask God to baptize you in His Spirit. Tell Him you feel strange about it (if you do) but that you're willing to yield to Him. Don't think it through, just begin to pray "in faith" that He is baptizing you. He won't open your mouth and start it for you. That's your part. But once you take that step of faith He will meet you there and take over. Just begin to worship Him in the Spirit. Pray in tongues, lift your hands, and let go and let God! And please tell us of your experience. Remember, don't seek tongues, seek the Giver. Ask God for the Gift of the Holy Spirit. Tongues will come with the gift. *(After the first printing of this book I have had testimonies of people getting baptized in the Spirit after reading this chapter. Don't be afraid. It's a beautiful honor and privilege to pray to God in the Spirit, in tongues).*

Ephesians 6:18a > *Praying at all times in the Spirit, with all prayer and supplication*

List 3 things you feel are important to learning to pray in the Spirit more often:

1. _____

2. _____

3. _____

Write down your "take-a-ways" from this lesson on Pray in the Spirit:

_____

_____

_____

_____

_____

Young man, the secret of my success is that at an early age I discovered I was not God.

– Oliver Wendell Holmes

Jesus! It is the name which moves the harps of heaven to melody . . . a gathering up of the hallelujahs of eternity in five letters.

– Charles Spurgeon

CHAPTER 9

Pray in the Authority of Christ

"Whatever you ask in my name [i.e. Authority], this I will do, that the Father may be glorified in the Son." (John 14:13)

As we dive even deeper into the various aspects of a strong effective prayer life, we find a powerful truth – answered prayer comes through acknowledging the authority of Christ. The authority is not derived from our own strength or merit but flows from our reverential relationship with Christ and confidence in His victory over sin and death. What does it mean to pray in the authority of Christ? And how does that empower our prayers?

Before we can effectively pray in the authority of Christ, we must first recognize the source of this authority. Jesus declared, "All authority in heaven and on earth has been given to me" (Matthew 28:18). This authority extends to every aspect of our lives, including our prayers. When we pray in the authority of Christ, we align ourselves with His divine power and sovereignty, knowing that He has conquered sin, death, and the powers of darkness.

An example of this type of authority is when one person (whom we'll refer to as the "giver") grants "power of attorney" to another (whom we'll refer to as the "receiver"). The power to grant this authority lies in the hands of the "giver." It is a decision the "giver" makes to entrust all that belongs to them to another person. The "receiver" has the responsibility to properly handle the "givers" estate in the same manner that the "giver" would if/until the "giver" returns to take back that authority. Jesus has entrusted us with the power to destroy the works of the devil and preach the kingdom. We are to do this in the same manner He did and continue doing so until He returns. Though we have been given "power of attorney," so to speak, we must be conscious of how we handle God's "business" and ever mindful to acknowledge that it is **His** power and authority and we are simply stewards of what He's entrusted to us. We are ambassadors of the Kingdom and are given the authority to represent said Kingdom; but, He remains the King.

Praying in the authority of Christ enables us to approach God with confidence and boldness. We can boldly come before the throne of grace, knowing that Jesus has paved the way for us through His sacrificial death and resurrection. Our prayers are not based on our own merit but on the finished work of Christ on the cross. With this understanding of Christ's authority, we can approach God with confidence and boldness, knowing that we are His beloved children and co-heirs with Christ (Romans 8:17). *"Therefore, since we have a great high priest who has ascended into heaven, Jesus the Son of God, let us hold firmly to the faith we profess. For we do not have a high priest who is unable to empathize with our weaknesses, but we have one who has been tempted in every way, just as we are—yet he did not sin. Let us then approach God's throne of grace with confidence, so that we may receive mercy and find grace to help us in our time of need"* (Hebrews 4:14-16, NIV).

When we pray in the authority of Christ, we can speak with power over circumstances in our lives and the lives of others. Matthew 21:21-22 shares a story of this authority of Christ that has been given to us. It reads, *"And Jesus answered them, 'Truly, I say to you, if you have faith and do not doubt, you will not only do what has been done to the fig tree, but even if you say to this mountain, 'Be taken up and thrown into the sea,' it will happen. And whatever you ask in prayer, you will receive, if you have faith.'"*

Just as Jesus demonstrated His authority over sickness, demons, and nature during His earthly ministry, He has given us the same authority to proclaim His kingdom and bring healing and restoration. We can speak with authority, knowing that our words are backed by the power of Christ Himself.

Praying in the authority of Christ also means praying according to God's will. Jesus taught His disciples to pray,

"Your kingdom come, your will be done, on earth as it is in heaven" (Matthew 6:10, NIV). As we align our prayers with God's will, we can trust that He will answer according to His perfect plan and purposes. *"This is the confidence we have in approaching God: that if we ask anything according to his will, he hears us. And if we know that he hears us—whatever we ask—we know that we have what we asked of him."* (1 John 5:14-15, NIV)

We are also empowered, through Christ's authority, to engage in spiritual warfare and overcome the forces of darkness. *"For our struggle is not against flesh and blood, but against the rulers, against the authorities, against the powers of this dark world and against the spiritual forces of evil in the heavenly realms."* (Ephesians 6:12, NIV) Jesus has given us authority to trample on snakes and scorpions and to overcome all the power of the enemy (Luke 10:19, NIV). Through prayer and the power of the Holy Spirit, we can stand firm against the schemes of the devil and advance God's kingdom on earth.

Praying in the authority of Christ is a powerful privilege given to every believer. By recognizing the source of authority, praying with confidence and boldness, speaking with authority over circumstances, aligning our prayers with God's will, and exercising authority in spiritual warfare, we can unleash the transformative power of prayer in our lives and in the world around us, bringing Heaven down to Earth!

So, concerning prayer, when you ask something, or make a request, from God, or make your "petitions" known, and you do so understanding and acknowledging that it is only because of Jesus that any of your prayers are answered, then you are praying in His Name, (i.e. in His authority). You can be assured that if Jesus signs the petition He will certainly honor His signature. He always backs up His Word and His promises.

Live Out Loud

Prayer:

Lord, all authority in Heaven and Earth belong to you! And you have given your followers your Holy Spirit and that same authority over sickness, disease, and every evil thing. Today, I am determined to pray in that authority. Not as though this authority comes from me but from You, Lord. And when I pray in the authority of Jesus Christ I know that you hear me and my prayers are answered, according to your will. Amen

Action:

Find someone who is in need of healing. Ask if you can pray for them. Then simply pray in the authority of Jesus Christ and watch God move in answer to your prayer. If you don't see immediate results, don't be discouraged. Keep believing!

Mark 16:17-18 (NLT) > *These miraculous signs will accompany those who believe: They will cast out demons <u>in my name</u>, and they will speak in new languages. They will be able to handle snakes with safety, and if they drink anything poisonous, it won't hurt them. They will be able to place their hands on the sick, and they will be healed.*

List 3 authoritative declarations from God's Word to help you stand in faith:

1. _____

2. _____

3. _____

Write down your "take-a-ways" from this lesson on Pray in the Authority of Christ:

_____

_____

_____

_____

_____

Your word is a lamp to my feet And a light to my path.

— Psalm 119:105 (NKJV)

Heaven and earth will pass away, but my words will never pass away.

— Matthew 24:35 (NIV)

God's laws are pure, eternal, just. They are more desirable than gold. They are sweeter than honey dripping from a honeycomb. For they warn us away from harm and give success to those who obey them.

— Psalm 119:9-11(TLB)

CHAPTER 10

Abide in the Word

If you abide in Me, and My words abide in you, you will ask what you desire, and it shall be done for you. (John 15:7 NKJV)

Most believers can quote this Bible verse, but how many are using it to secure answers to their requests? Jesus makes clear provision here for having our prayers answered – by abiding in His Word.

"Abide." It's a word we seldom hear and rarely use in everyday language. Yet, I've found it to be somewhat of a master key—a key that unlocks all doors, especially when other keys seem ineffective. Prayer is powerful, important, and our means of communication with God. Through prayer, we can agree with and believe for each other, witnessing God's miraculous work in our lives. Prayer can help us live the extraordinary life. Therefore, it is vital that we understand this 'master key' to answered prayer.

Let's delve into the structure of this passage before exploring its deeper meaning. *"If you abide in Me, and My words abide in you, you will ask what you desire, and it shall be done for you."* (John 15:7 NKJV). Jesus speaks here, presenting an "if, then" statement—a cause and effect scenario. "If" signifies a condition, and "then" indicates the result. We can rely on these cause-and-effect statements, confident that the outcome will materialize if the condition is met.

God's promises are sure—they are "Yes" and "Amen" in Him. His Word accomplishes what it is sent to do. Some promises are fulfilled simply because God loves His children and keeps His Word. Others require our participation; when we fulfill the conditions (the "if"), God fulfills His promises (the "then").

Let me explain this another way: We understand 'requirements.' We have requirements every day. It may be for our job, in our home, with our kids, etc. The law itself puts 'requirements' on us. If we don't want to get into a car wreck, then we don't run a red light. If we want to get a new house, then we have to prove our income. Sometimes when we apply for certain things, then we have to prove we have a place of employment. So there are always requirements. We're used to requirements. But oftentimes, because we've accepted God's grace, we think He no longer has any "requirements of us." Granted, we are saved by grace, through faith, and none of our own doing, so that we don't get into boasting; but that doesn't mean God doesn't have requirements of us. The Bible even mentions leaders, as well as lay persons, having requirements. Some requisites may be just simply to live holy, or, like Jesus said, love God and love others as you love yourself, fulfilling the whole law. Others may be in reference to certain positions of authority within the Church. We can see through these examples that requirements are still in the Word of God. And we recognize many of these requirements through 'if, then' statements. Even if the word 'then' isn't used, it's understood. Here in this text, Jesus says, "*If you abide in Me and My words abide in you . . .* [understood 'then'] *you can ask whatever you desire and it will be done for you.*" The second part of this promise is the result of fulfilling the first part. If you abide, then you can ask, and it will be done for you. Not 'it might be;' it will be.

Now, let's take a moment and ask ourselves, "Do I want the desires of my heart to come to fruition? Do I want my prayers to be answered and God's promises to be fulfilled in my life?" (I'm sure we can all answer "yes" to those questions). Well, if we want this, then we need to do what the first part says in order to get the last part to be fulfilled, right? The master key to having our prayers answered, being effective in prayer, and praying Heaven down to Earth is to abide in Him and allow His Word to abide in us.

But what exactly does it mean to "abide?" The definition for abide is to "remain, continue; dwell; be present; endure; stand; wait for; accept without opposition or question; to remain steadfast or faithful to; to keep." It also connotes "live." So, if you're present with God, if you wait on God, if you endure in God (because some people fall away), if you live in Him, (live doesn't mean to stay for a couple days – live means live!); then you will have your requests fulfilled. Jesus said if you remain faithful to Him, enduring in Him, AND IF His Word*s* are kept, dwell in you, and are accepted without opposition or question, THEN you may ask *whatever* you want and it will be done for you. Again, earlier in verse 5 of John, chapter 15, Jesus said that He is the Vine and we are the branches and that if we abide in Him then we will bear much fruit because without Him we can do nothing. If we live and remain in Him, we *will* bear fruit.

Not only are we to abide in Him but we are to allow His Word to abide in us. If His Word, or "*remata*," (where we get the word Rhema, or spoken word), abides in us, then we can ask whatever we desire and it will be done. Now, today we often hear alot about a "prophetic" word being a Rhema word; but in this particular text of scripture, and the context of what he's talking about, it actually means "a thing spoken by the living voice, not a dead voice." It's a *living* voice. Jesus is the Word. He's life. So, He's talking about abiding in Him and allowing His teachings to abide, live, be present, stay in, us. The teachings of Christ are the things that He spoke. His living voice. It's a word that produces faith. It means "something has established itself permanently within my soul and always exerts its power in me." That is what He's talking about here! The Rhema word is "something that has established itself within my soul permanently and always exerts its power in me." The Words of Jesus are alive! The Holy Spirit has established Himself permanently within my soul and exerts the power of faith in me to believe God. The Holy Spirit is our Rhema; our living voice! He is the Word that has come to live on the inside of us.

We want the teachings of Christ to come and dwell permanently within us. We want to be living epistles! As the "rhema" comes to be always present within us, we can then allow that power of the Holy Spirit, of faith, to move through us. As we abide in Christ, and His teachings abide in us, THEN we can ask whatever we *desire* and it will be done. This word, desire, means "wanting what is best or optimal because someone is ready and willing to act." Whew! I love that! That is such a powerful definition. It means to "act in accordance with a rule or a decision or a recommendation." This word (thelete) is commonly used of the Lord "extending his best offer to the believer." When this text talks about the desires of your heart, God is putting His best offer on the table. He's offering something that is His best. It means to ask God for His best and most optimal AND says that we are ready and willing to act upon it. This understanding goes even further. What is that rule or decision? What is that recommendation? It's that God wants "to birth His persuasion, His faith, in us." In other words, as we abide in Him and His Word abides in us, we can ask for God's best; and if we are ready and willing to act on it, we will cause faith to rise in us to believe that it will be done. There's so much more to learn when you start really studying the context of scripture. This is powerful if you understand it fully. In essence, when we "ask and receive," we are seeking what God considers best and optimal for us. It is an acknowledgment that His plans far surpass our own, and it requires a readiness to act in accordance with His will. So let us be diligent in seeking God's best for our lives and be ever ready and willing to follow His lead.

Here's a master key: abiding in Christ and allowing Christ to abide in you. It's about inviting Him to continually dwell within you, establishing a constant connection between you and God. This connection enables you to ask for anything—not just some things, but anything. This does not mean that we can ask for frivolous or selfish desires. Rather, it speaks to the importance of aligning our desires with God's will and being ready and willing to act upon His promptings.

God's best offer is unparalleled. Even our best efforts pale in comparison to His best for us. When we abide in Him, He grants us the desires of our hearts, persuading us with His optimal plan. All He asks is that we are ready and willing to act.

When God promises that "it will be done," it signifies a profound transformation. His blessings transcend earthly limitations; they come from another realm entirely. While earthly riches may pale in comparison, God's blessings bring wholeness, health, joy, and love from heaven down to earth.

Consider the prayer Jesus taught His disciples: "thy will be done on Earth as it is in heaven." This isn't a plea for the kingdom to come from heaven to earth; rather, it's an invitation for the kingdom within us to manifest itself outwardly. We are vessels of this heavenly kingdom, called to bring its reality into the earthly realm.

This transition from heavenly to earthly manifestation implies movement, growth, and action. It's about God's actions emerging from eternity into time, bringing His plans to fruition in our lives.

So, let's embrace this transition, allowing God's best to manifest in our lives as we align our desires with His will. Let's walk as citizens of heaven, bringing the reality of God's kingdom to earth by praying from a place called "abide."

Live Out Loud

Prayer:

Lord, it is a blessing to have your Word. I choose to show my gratitude for your Word by daily reading and meditating on it. I trust that you will answer my prayers because I choose to live in You and allow your teachings to live in me.

Action:

Do a similar exercise to chapter 8. Only this time just study God's Word, separating/consecrating yourself from the World and just resting in His Word. Do this daily, focusing on the Word and putting it in your heart -- allowing Jesus to live through you.

John 15:8 > *"By this my Father is glorified, that you bear much fruit and so prove to be my disciples."*

Joshua 1:8 > "This Book of the Law shall not depart from your mouth, but you shall meditate on it day and night, so that you may be careful to do according to all that is written in it. For then you will make your way prosperous, and then you will have good success."

List 3 things you can do to show that you are "abiding" in Christ:

1. _____

2. _____

3. _____

Write down your "take-a-ways" from this lesson on Abide in the Word:

_____

_____

_____

_____

_____

But if we are living in the light of God's presence, just as Jesus does, then we have wonderful fellowship and joy with each other . . .

— 1 John 1:7 (TLB)

A person standing alone can be attacked and defeated, but two can stand back-to-back and conquer. Three are even better, for a triple-braided cord is not easily broken.

— Ecclesiastes 4:12 (NLT)

CHAPTER 11

Pray with Others

"Again I say to you, if two of you agree on earth about anything they ask, it will be done for them by my Father in heaven." (Mt. 18:19)

This isn't just about throwing a couple of prayers together; it's about tapping into the immense power of agreement. God, by His very nature, is a God of unity. He delights in fellowship and harmony, embodying the perfect unity of the Trinity. As Jesus prayed in John 17:21, when we come together as one, with a shared purpose and vision, our prayers become a symphony that resonates in the heavens.

Consider the early believers in Acts, gathered together in one accord, praying fervently in unity. It was in that atmosphere of agreement that the Holy Spirit moved in power, igniting the flame of revival that would spread throughout the world. And that was just the beginning. When we align our hearts and minds with others in prayer, we create a spiritual synergy that amplifies the effectiveness of our petitions. Together, we become co-laborers with God, partners in His Kingdom work.

When we join our faith with others', the power of our prayers skyrockets. It's like combining forces in a spiritual powerhouse, where each believer's faith adds fuel to the fire of collective intercession. In this way, our prayers become unstoppable forces for change in the spiritual realm and on the earthly plane.

So, how do we harness this power of agreement in our own lives? Seek out fellow believers who are strong in faith and join forces with them in prayer. Share with them the insights and revelations you've gained about prayer, inviting them to add their faith to yours and release a torrent of angelic forces on your behalf. This isn't just about finding prayer partners; it's about building a community of believers who are committed to lifting each other up in prayer, standing in agreement for breakthrough and victory in every area of life.

Now, let's be real—it's not always easy to pray with others. We all come from different backgrounds, with different perspectives and approaches to prayer. But that's no excuse to go it alone. Find someone, a group, a community—whatever it takes—to come together in prayer. It might require stepping out of your comfort zone, but the rewards are worth it. When we lay aside our differences and unite in prayer, we create a powerful spiritual synergy that transcends individual limitations and ushers in the miraculous.

I believe it's high time for churches and ministries to prioritize prayer, and especially to cultivate a culture of agreement and unity. This book could serve as a launching pad, a guide to help us align our prayers with the heart of God. As Proverbs 4:7 (KJV) reminds us, *"In all your getting, get understanding."* When we all operate from the same playbook, there's no limit to what God can do through our prayers. Let's commit to coming together in prayer, to seek God's face with one voice and one heart, and watch as He moves mountains in response to our collective faith.

Together, we can break through the toughest strongholds, lifting each other up and carrying the weight of our prayers with ease. So let's build our spiritual muscles, strengthen our unity, and watch as God moves mountains in response to our collective faith.

Live Out Loud

Prayer:

Dear Jesus, thank you for the blessing of relationship, of agreement, and of covenant. Help me connect with like-minded people to agree in prayer for your will to be done. Amen

Action:

Set a time to pray with various individuals and/or with a group. Maybe even lead a prayer group. Get a focus and dispatch the angels to carry out the request. It can be a group that meets on a regular basis or you could just find people to agree with you about a specific need in an individual's life or even in the community or nation you live.

Matthew 18:20 > "For where two or three are gathered in my name, there am I among them."

Acts 4:32a (KJV) > "And the multitude of them that believed were of one heart and one soul."

List 3 people you can contact to pray for regarding a need and pray, believing in the authority given through Christ Jesus:

1. _____

2. _____

3. _____

Write down your "take-a-ways" from this lesson on Pray in the Authority of Christ:

_____

_____

_____

_____

_____

Prayer is not overcoming God's reluctance; it is laying hold of His highest willingness.

– R. C. Trench

God Almighty does not throw dice.

– Albert Einstein

CHAPTER 12

Understanding the Will and Sovereignty of God

And all the inhabitants of the earth are reputed as nothing: and He does according to His will in the army of heaven, and among the inhabitants of the earth: and none can stay His hand, or say unto Him, What are You doing? (Dan. 4:35, KJV)

Whatever the Lord pleased, He did in heaven, and in earth, in the seas, and all deep places. (Ps. 135:6, NKJV)

Both riches and honor come from You, and you reign over all; and in Your hand is power and might; and in Your hand it is to make great, and to give strength unto all. (1 Chr. 29:12, KJV)

Ever found yourself pouring your heart out to God, only to be met with silence? It's a scene familiar to many believers. Despite our heartfelt prayers and unwavering faith, there are moments when it feels like our petitions hit a wall. In those times, doubt creeps in, and we wonder if God hears us, if He truly cares.

But in the midst of our uncertainties lies a truth we can't afford to overlook: the will and sovereignty of God. These foundational truths shape the very fabric of our prayer life, guiding us through its highs and lows.

Without grasping the depth of God's sovereignty, we risk stumbling through our prayer journey, unsure of why some prayers seemingly go unanswered. We may even question God's character, wondering why He allows circumstances to unfold in ways that defy our expectations. But the reality is that God's will reigns supreme over every aspect of our lives, prayer included.

To understand God's sovereignty is to delve into the essence of His being. It's about recognizing His absolute authority over all creation, from the grandest cosmic events to the tiniest details of our lives. Nothing escapes His notice, and His plans always come to fruition, even when they don't align with our desires.

Similarly, His will encompasses His perfect purpose for His creation. While we may pray fervently for specific outcomes, God's will surpasses our limited perspective, guided by His divine wisdom and overarching plan for humanity. Surrendering to His will means trusting that His ways are higher than ours, even when they lead us down unexpected paths.

Some years ago, I faced a particular situation in my life where I prayed fervently, believing that God would answer and bring about the desired outcome. He had always been faithful in answering my prayers, so I approached this situation with unwavering faith. However, things did not unfold as I had hoped. For the first time in my Christian journey, I felt a surge of anger towards God bubbling up within me. I wrestled with these feelings, questioning why God wouldn't grant my request. Wouldn't a "yes" from Him align with His loving and just nature? These thoughts weighed heavily on my heart.

But just as I began to lean towards anger, God intervened in a surprising way. I stumbled upon an online message from a pastor discussing the dangers of harboring anger towards God. It was a divine encounter—I rarely tuned in to his teachings, yet on that day, his message spoke directly to my situation. It was a powerful reminder of God's presence and guidance in the midst of our struggles. Recognizing the warning, I humbled myself and quickly repented.

Some may argue that it's acceptable to express anger towards God. And while it's true that God can handle our emotions, displaying anger towards Him reveals a fundamental misunderstanding of His sovereignty. As He reminded Job, who are we to question the Creator of the universe? (Job 38:4). Instead of yielding to anger, let us humbly submit to God's authority, trusting in His perfect wisdom and plan for our lives.

If you delve into the conclusion of the book of Job, you'll gain a deeper understanding and appreciation for God's sovereignty. In the Kingdom of God, we don't assert our "rights;" rather, we recognize and cherish the privileges bestowed upon us. While we may struggle to comprehend God's justice and His decisions regarding our prayers, we can rest assured that He is always on our side. In His omniscience, He knows what's best for us. Trusting Him means facing every challenge knowing He is in control, even when it's not easy.

I've been holding onto a specific request from God for over five years now, and I've yet to see it come to fruition. Despite this, I firmly believe in His promise and His will for my situation—a resounding "yes" and "amen." Even in the waiting room of uncertainty, God remains sovereign.

God's sovereignty is intricately linked with His will. While He has granted us free will, our choices are often influenced by our sinful nature unless we willingly submit to God's will. Despite His sovereignty, God doesn't compel us to comply with His will. This is why we sometimes witness events that we struggle to comprehend, leading us to blame God for not intervening. However, God respects our autonomy and won't override our will, even though He has the power to do so.

In prayer, it's crucial to discern God's will for a given situation. While it is His will to heal every time, there may be factors we haven't considered. Studying Scripture and seeking His guidance can illuminate His will. For instance, Jeremiah 29:11 assures us of God's plans to bless and prosper us, giving us hope and a future. Armed with this knowledge, we can pray confidently, knowing that God hears and answers our prayers according to His will.

As we understand the will and sovereignty of God in our prayer time, let's reflect on the profound example set by Jesus Himself. In the garden of Gethsemane, faced with the weight of the cross and the impending agony that awaited Him, Jesus prayed, "Father, if it is Your will, take this cup away from Me; nevertheless not My will, but Yours, be done" (Luke 22:42, NKJV). In this moment of intense anguish, Jesus exemplified the essence of submission to God's will. Despite His human desire to avoid suffering, He yielded Himself completely to the Father's plan. Likewise, as we navigate the complexities of prayer, may we echo Jesus' surrender, trusting in the sovereignty of God even when our own desires may differ. Let us pray with hearts aligned with His will, knowing that His purposes are perfect and His plans are ultimately for our good.

Live Out Loud

Prayer:

Lord, I trust in you. You alone are sovereign. In every situation in life help me to always remember that you are in control and have the best outcome planned for me. I surrender to your will, Lord, not mine. Amen

Action:

Choose something about which you're unsure as to whether or not it is God's will (a general topic like divorce, holy living, or healing). Look up this word, or related words, in your Bible or online. See if you can find God's will concerning it. (Keep in mind that we are under grace and not the law and that our own will plays a part in what takes place in the world around us).

De. 4:39 (KJV) > *Know therefore this day, and consider it in your heart, that the Lord He is God in heaven above, and upon the earth beneath: there is none else.*

Ps. 83:18 (KJV) > *That men may know that You, whose name alone is JEHOVAH, are the Most High over all the earth.*

Ac. 17:24-25 (KJV) > *God that made the world and all things therein, seeing that He is Lord of heaven and earth, dwells not in temples made with hands; neither is worshiped* with men's hands, as though He needs anything, seeing He gives to all life, and breath, and all things;

Job 42:2 >>> *I know you can do all things, and no purpose of yours can be thwarted.*

List 3 verses within this chapter that you can meditate on and remember when in prayer.

1._____

2._____

3._____

Write down your "take-a-ways" from this lesson on Pray in the Authority of Christ:

_____

_____

_____

_____

_____

APPENDIX A

What About Favor?

In the beautiful tapestry of answered prayers, God's favor is like a warm embrace, showering blessings and shielding us from harm. Favor can sometimes be earned through faithfulness and obedience, or it can be freely given, like a precious gift of grace from God.

Favor plays a big part in answered prayers. Sometimes, it's because of our strong belief, aligning with what God wants, or for reasons we may not fully understand. There are moments when God surprises us with blessings out of the blue, simply because He loves us.

The Bible tells us about people who walked in favor with both God and others. Jesus himself is described as having favor with both God and people (Luke 2:52), and so was Stephen (Acts 6:8), known for his unwavering faith. And upon Mary was bestowed the acknowledgment of being "highly favored . . . and blessed" (Luke 1:28). Maybe it's because their hearts were firmly set on God, and they never wavered in their devotion. Or perhaps, like the Apostle Paul, they were simply chosen by God for a special purpose.

But here's the thing about favor—it can sometimes make others jealous or resentful. While we can earn favor with people through things like our skills or how we look, God's favor is different. It's a gift from Him, something we can't earn or control.

So whether we find ourselves surrounded by God's favor or longing for it, prayer remains our strongest weapon. We can ask God for His favor in our lives, knowing that He listens and responds according to His perfect plan. So let's keep praying, trusting that God's favor is always within reach.

God blesses the righteous and surrounds them with favor.

— Psalm 5:12

God opposes the proud but shows favor to the humble.

— James 4:6

I will do everything you ask because I am pleased with you.

— Exodus 33:17

Have love and faithfulness . . . then you will find favor and a good name in the sight of God and man.

— Proverbs 3:3-4

APPENDIX B

What About Humility?

This is a challenging aspect of prayer for those who understand the power of faith in prayer. To be confident that God will answer your prayer, while remaining humble and realizing the answer lies in His power, is a balance to achieve. Faith without humility can lead to arrogance, where we begin to believe that our prayers are answered because of our own righteousness or eloquence. On the other hand, humility without faith can result in a lack of confidence, making us hesitant to approach God boldly. Balancing these two aspects requires a deep trust in God's character and promises, recognizing that He is both willing and able to respond to our prayers while maintaining a posture of reverence and dependence on Him.

Isaiah 66:2 says that God looks to the man "who is humble and contrite in spirit and trembles at [*His*] word." Satan fell from Heaven because of pride, the opposite of humility. Jesus said He came to serve, not to be served. He humbled Himself. This contrast between pride and humility is stark and instructive. Satan's downfall reminds us of the destructive power of pride, which blinds us to our need for God and leads to rebellion. In contrast, Jesus' life exemplifies perfect humility and submission to the Father's will, showing us that true greatness in God's kingdom comes through servanthood and self-sacrifice. By embracing humility, we open ourselves to God's grace and favor, positioning ourselves to receive His blessings and guidance.

No one should "humble" us. That's called humiliation. We must, like Jesus, take the responsibility of humbling ourselves. God says in 2 Chronicles 7:14, "If my people who are called by my name humble themselves, and pray and seek my face and turn from their wicked ways, then I will hear from heaven and will forgive their sin and heal their land." Humility is an absolute necessity in prayer. It is an intentional act, a choice we make to acknowledge our limitations and our need for God's intervention. When we humble ourselves, we create space for God's power to work in and through us. This deliberate act of lowering ourselves before God is not about self-deprecation but about recognizing His greatness and our dependence on His mercy and grace. It is a posture that invites divine intervention and aligns us with God's purposes.

Humility is not about going around with a "such a worm as I" mentality. Once we've received Christ, we are no longer sinners in our identity; we are children of God. Thus, we don't approach God in prayer labeling ourselves as mere sinners. However, we must understand our position as creation, not the Creator. We must realize we can do nothing apart from Christ. It is only by His grace that we are allowed the privilege to even speak to Him. So, we humble ourselves while at the same time coming "boldly to the throne of grace" (Hebrews 4:16, KJV). This dynamic of humility and boldness reflects a mature faith that understands our worth and identity in Christ while acknowledging our complete reliance on His grace. By approaching God with this balanced mindset, we honor Him as our loving Father who desires to hear from His children and respond to their needs, while also submitting to His divine wisdom and authority. This dual posture enables us to experience the fullness of God's presence and power in our lives, transforming our prayers into powerful conversations that align with His will.

This bold humility is the key to powerful prayer. Be confident in His authority and your faith. Approach God with the assurance that He hears you and will answer according to His will. But remain humble, acknowledging your dependence on His power and grace.

As you pray, remember that it's not about the eloquence of your words or the intensity of your plea. It's about the posture of your heart. When we humble ourselves, we align with God's heart. He delights in our submission and dependence on Him. This humility is not a sign of weakness but a reflection of our trust in God's strength.

Jesus, our ultimate example, demonstrated this balance perfectly. Despite His divine nature, He chose to serve and humble Himself, even to the point of death on a cross (Philippians 2:8). In our prayers, we must emulate this humility. We must come before God with a sincere recognition of His sovereignty and our reliance on Him.

Moreover, humility in prayer invites God's presence into our lives in a transformative way. It opens the door for God to work mightily within us and through us. When we humble ourselves, we allow God to lift us up, to exalt us in His perfect timing (James 4:10).

So, approach prayer with a heart full of faith and a spirit of humility. Boldly ask for God's intervention, confident that He hears and will act. But always remember to submit to His will, trusting that His plans are greater than ours. In this balance of bold faith and humble submission, we find the true power of prayer.

Reflect upon your present blessings, of which every man has many; not on your past misfortunes, of which all men have some.

— Charles Dickens

The sufficiency of my merit is to know that my merit is not sufficient.

— St. Augustine

Those who travel the high road of humility are not troubled by heavy traffic.

— Alan K. Simpson

APPENDIX C

What About Fasting?

In Matthew 17:21, we are presented with an intense scene where a distressed father brings his afflicted son to Jesus, seeking healing. The boy suffers from severe seizures, often endangering his life by throwing him into fire or water. Despite the disciples' efforts, they couldn't alleviate the boy's torment.

Jesus' response to the disciples' inability to heal the boy sheds light on the situation. He first addresses their faith, highlighting the lack thereof. When they inquire about their failure, Jesus pinpoints the root cause, stating, "Because of your unbelief." He then adds that fasting and prayer are required for such situations.

How can fasting help cast out a demon? Demons come out by the authority of Christ. But this demon would not relent. Some teachers of the Word say that when Jesus says this "kind" that He is referring to the kind of unbelief that the disciples had. However, the word "kind" here in the Greek is referring to a "species." So, Jesus is saying that this type of demon only comes out by fasting and prayer. We're not told exactly what "kind" he means – perhaps it is strong, one of the mind, or maybe has been there for a long time. We don't know. But we do know that if a demonic spirit is resisting the command of the believer then perhaps fasting is required. Rather than focusing solely on the nature of the demon, Jesus is most likely emphasizing the disciples' need for increased faith. Fasting helps to grow our faith and to believe that all demonic "species" must obey the authority of Christ given to those who believe.

The principle of fasting and prayer remains invaluable in our pursuit of effective prayer. Fasting elevates our spirits, empowering us with faith and spiritual authority. Just as Jesus fasted before embarking on His ministry, fasting can enhance our effectiveness in prayer and spiritual warfare.

Combining fasting with prayer can yield remarkable results. I've personally witnessed the transformative power of fasting and prayer, where individuals have experienced salvation and miraculous breakthroughs. By setting aside worldly distractions and devoting ourselves to seeking God's presence through fasting and prayer, we position ourselves for divine intervention and greater effectiveness in our prayer lives, thereby causing Heaven to come down and invade this earthly plane.

Here are some additional insights on how fasting can enrich our prayer life and lead to the desired outcomes:

1. **Heightened Spiritual Sensitivity:** Fasting sensitizes us to the leading of the Holy Spirit and helps us discern God's voice more clearly. When we abstain from food or other distractions, our spiritual senses become sharper, enabling us to align our prayers with God's will more effectively. Isaiah 58:11 shares the types of blessings that come after practicing the fast that pleases God - *"And the Lord will guide you continually and satisfy your desire in scorched places and make your bones strong; and you shall be like a watered garden, like a spring of water, whose waters do not fail."*

2. **Increased Focus and Devotion:** Fasting redirects our attention from worldly concerns to seeking God's face. By sacrificing physical nourishment, we demonstrate our earnest desire to commune with God and prioritize His presence above all else. This heightened focus cultivates a deeper sense of devotion in our prayer life. Joel 2:12 - *"Now, therefore,"* says the Lord, *"Turn to Me with all your heart, with fasting, with weeping, and with mourning."*

3. **Breaking Strongholds:** Fasting can break spiritual strongholds and barriers hindering the manifestation of answered prayers. As we deny our fleshly desires through fasting, we weaken the grip of worldly distractions and sinful patterns, creating an

environment conducive to spiritual breakthroughs. Matthew 17:21 (NKJV) - *"However, this kind does not go out except by prayer and fasting."* Isaiah 58:6 (NKJV) - *"Is this not the fast that I have chosen: to loose the bonds of wickedness, to undo the heavy burdens, to let the oppressed go free, and that you break every yoke?"*

4. **Cultivating Humility and Dependency:** Fasting humbles us before God and acknowledges our dependence on Him for sustenance and strength. In our weakness, God's power is made perfect, and He delights in pouring out His grace and favor on those who humble themselves before Him. James 4:10 - *"Humble yourselves before the Lord, and He will exalt you"*

5. **Accelerating Spiritual Growth:** Fasting accelerates our spiritual growth by fostering intimacy with God and deepening our understanding of His Word. As we seek God's face in prayer and fasting, we are transformed from glory to glory, becoming more aligned with His purposes and desires. 2 Corinthians 3:18 (NKJV)- *"But we all, with unveiled faces, beholding as in a mirror the glory of the Lord, are being transformed into the same image from glory to glory, just as by the Spirit of the Lord."* This is how I received the baptism of the Holy Spirit. I fasted with nothing for 3 days (I wasn't aware at the time that I

should at least be drinking water). By the second day the Lord answered me in a profound way and I was filled to overflow with God's Spirit.

Incorporating fasting into our prayer life requires intentionality and discipline, but the rewards are immeasurable. By fasting and praying fervently, we position ourselves to experience God's presence in a profound way and witness His miraculous intervention in response to our heartfelt petitions. It is a powerful spiritual discipline that can deepen our intimacy with God and enhance the effectiveness of our prayers.

And now about fasting – When you fast, declining your food for a spiritual purpose, don't do it publicly, as the hypocrites do . . .

– Matthew 6:16 (TLB)

The best of all medicines are resting and fasting.

– Benjamin Franklin

Conclusion

L et's take a moment to reflect on the powerful truths and practical insights we've uncovered about prayer. We've seen that prayer is our direct line of communication with God, our way to bring heaven's influence down to earth. In these chaotic and corrupt times, effective prayer is more crucial than ever.

Throughout this book, we've explored the essential elements of prayer: the necessity of it, the matters of the heart, and the incredible value it holds. We've learned how to pray in righteousness, with passion, meaningful intent, and unwavering faith. We've embraced the importance of praying in the Spirit, standing in the authority of Christ, and abiding in His Word. We've discovered the strength in praying with others and the significance of understanding God's will and sovereignty.

Each chapter has aimed to give you the tools and understanding needed to make your prayers powerful and effective. Whether it's invoking God's favor, combining fasting with prayer, or grasping the dynamics of effective prayer, the goal has been to empower you to see real, tangible results in your prayer life.

Prayer isn't just a religious duty or a ritual. It's a vibrant, life-giving conversation with the Creator of the Universe. It's where we align our hearts with God's will, allowing His plans and purposes to manifest in our lives. Through prayer, we co-create with God, shaping our present and future according to His divine blueprint. It is an exciting opportunity and privilege given to us by Jesus Christ and operating through us by the Holy Spirit.

As you continue this walk of faith and commit to pray without ceasing, my hope is that you take these principles to heart. Let them transform your approach to prayer, making it a dynamic and effective practice in your daily life. Approach God with confidence, knowing He hears you and is eager to respond. Stay persistent, be patient, and trust in His perfect timing.

Expect to see heaven come down in your life, as you grow in these principles of prayer. Look for the praise reports, the miracles, and the breakthroughs. Share your stories, encourage others, and let the power of prayer ripple through your community and beyond.

Thank you for joining me on this transformative journey. May your prayers rise like sweet incense before God's throne, and may you witness His glory manifest on earth as it is in heaven. Now, go forth, pray with intention, and watch God move mightily on your behalf. Heaven is indeed coming down to earth, and you have the privilege of being a part of it.

Blessings and answered prayers,

Kim Robbins

Final Thoughts from the Author

I hope this book has been a blessing to you. I wanted to simplify the Believer's prayer life by giving some basic instructions that all of us can easily understand and adhere to. This is by no means an exhaustive list of principles that should govern our prayers. However, I believe it's a good start for those who are just learning how to build a relationship with God through prayer, as well as for those who desire God to answer specific prayers. If you would like to be informed about other books as they become available please visit www.kimrobbins.org.

We'd also love to hear of how this book has impacted your prayer life and any praise reports of answered prayer that you'd like to share. You can leave your e-mail address on the prayer closet page of my website. I look forward to hearing about the answers to your prayers!

You can also e-mail us at
admin@kimrobbins.org
Or
write to us at:

Kim Robbins Ministries
2095 Hwy 211 NW, Suite 2-F #306
Braselton, GA 30517

Kim Robbins

About the Author

Kim is a passionate speaker, author, YouTuber, and transformation/mindset coach. With a Master of Divinity from Oral Roberts University and ministry experience since 1991, Kim has pastored and co-pastored, sharing God's love and practical applications of His Word.

Known for her revelatory, dynamic, and humorous messages, Kim creates online courses and YouTube content to help listeners transform their lives (Romans 12:2). She has established two churches, two businesses, and her non-profit ministry, while also serving as the Executive Director of Spirit Life Center, a collaborative ministry offering spiritual education.

Kim lives just outside of Atlanta, GA with her husband, Lee, and their three adult children, Janae, Jordan, and Judah. She continues to inspire audiences through her teachings and compassionate outreach. She is currently expanding her reach through speaking engagements, writing books, developing online courses, and increasing the impact of her ministry outreach.

For more information or to book Kim for your next event, visit KimRobbins.org.

CONNECT with
Kim

YouTube
@KimRobbins

Facebook
Kim Robbins Ministries

Instagram
Kim Robbins Ministries

Tik Tok
@kimrobbins777

Pinterest
Kim Robbins

X
@Pastor Kim

Subscribe to the Podcast at
www.youtube.com/@KimRobbins

For Further Resources or to Subscribe to Kim's
Newsletter visit www.kimrobbins.org

www.ingramcontent.com/pod-product-compliance
Lightning Source LLC
Chambersburg PA
CBHW041628140626
46547CB00031B/1261